'S UNIVERSITY COLLEGE

BY

HEINEMANN Profiles

Elvis Presley

Rupert Matthews

Heinemann LIBRARY

H **www.heinemann.co.uk**
Visit our website to find out more information about **Heinemann Library** books.

To order:
☎ Phone 44 (0) 1865 888066
▤ Send a fax to 44 (0) 1865 314091
▯ Visit the Heinemann Bookshop at www.heinemann.co.uk to browse our catalogue and order online.

First published in Great Britain by Heinemann Library, Halley Court, Jordan Hill, Oxford OX2 8EJ, a division of Reed Educational and Professional Publishing Ltd.
Heinemann is a registered trademark of Reed Educational & Professional Publishing Limited.

OXFORD MELBOURNE AUCKLAND JOHANNESBURG BLANTYRE GABORONE IBADAN PORTSMOUTH NH (USA) CHICAGO

Produced for Heinemann Library by Discovery Books Limited
Edited by Rosemary William
Designed by Ian Winton
Originated by Dot Gradations
Printed and bound in Hong Kong/China

ISBN 0 431 08647 8

05 04 03 02 01
10 9 8 7 6 5 4 3 2 1

British Library Cataloguing in Publication Data

Matthews, Rupert
Elvis Presley. – (Heinemann profiles)
1. Presley, Elvis, 1935-1977 – Juvenile literature 2. Rock musicians –
    United States – Biography – Juvenile literature 3. Singers – United
    States – Biography – Juvenile Literature
I. Title
782.4'2'166'092

Acknowledgements
The Publishers would like to thank the following for permission to reproduce photographs: Corbis pp6, 7, 27, 30, 34, 46, 47, 48, 51; Peter Newark's American Pictures p22; Popperfoto pp20, 25, 35; Redferns pp4, 5, 9, 10, 11, 13, 14, 17, 18, 29, 31, 32, 37, 39, 41, 42, 45; Topham Picture Point pp28, 38.

Cover photograph reproduced with permission of Redferns

Every effort has been made to contact copyright holders of any material reproduced in this book. Any omissions will be rectified in subsequent printings if notice is given to the Publisher.

Any words appearing in the text in bold, **like this**, are explained in the Glossary.

CONTENTS

WHO WAS ELVIS PRESLEY?

Elvis Presley was called the 'King of **Rock and Roll**'. His distinctive voice redefined popular music for a generation and he set the pace for other performers who entered the world of pop music.

Elvis grew up in the poor area of a poor town, but his talent became obvious at a young age. From singing at church services, revival meetings and school concerts, Elvis went on to perform at local halls and soared to national fame when still a teenager.

Elvis performs on his 1968 NBC Television Special.

Before long his face was being seen on record covers, television shows, films, key rings, watches, mugs and playing cards. No singer before Elvis had achieved such enormous fame.

After 1961 Elvis's career got stuck in a rut as he concentrated on making a series of bland but popular films. These films were hardly impressive, but the music was often superb and he made a lot of money. When he returned to the stage in 1968 Elvis proved he was as dynamic as ever, but before long, binge eating, a lack of sleep and abuse of **prescription drugs** wrecked Elvis's health. In 1977 at the age of just 42 Elvis Presley died.

But Elvis the rock legend lives on. His music continues to make huge sales and his films are shown on television around the world. Some people refuse to believe that Elvis died so young and think he is living quietly in hiding somewhere. Elvis built up a legend that has survived long after his death.

'When we were kids, all we ever wanted to be was Elvis Presley.'
Paul McCartney, former member of the Beatles

A youthful Elvis Presley as commemorated on an American postage stamp.

29 USA

ROCK & ROLL SINGER, 1935-1977

ELVIS

Boy in Tupelo

Elvis Presley was born on 8 January 1935 in the small town of East Tupelo in the state of Mississippi in the southern USA. His twin brother, Jesse Garon Presley, died at birth and was buried the next day. Elvis's parents, Vernon and Gladys, had married two years earlier when aged just 17 and 21. They were poor but respectable, so Elvis's childhood would be a long struggle against poverty.

The house in which Elvis was born had been built by his father and some relatives in the garden of Elvis's grandfather's house. The house measured just 9 metres by 3 metres.

The two-room house in East Tupelo, Mississippi, where Elvis was born and lived until the age of thirteen.

BIRTHPLACE OF
ELVIS PRESLEY

Elvis Aaron Presley was born
Jan. 8, 1935, in this house,
built by his father. Presley's
career as a singer and enter-
tainer redefined American
popular music. He died Aug. 16,
1977, at Memphis, Tennessee.

**Elvis at the age
of three.**

Vernon Presley had a series of poorly paid jobs,
while Gladys helped earn money by taking on
sewing or cleaning work for wealthy local families.
Despite their money troubles, the Presleys always
found time for religion and it was at church that
Elvis first showed his musical talents. By the age of
three Elvis had learnt the words and tunes to the
more popular hymns, and would sing along to them
and dance up and down the aisles.

EARLY INFLUENCES

Elvis loved church music and was particularly drawn to the African-American churches, but because he was white, Elvis was not always welcome and sometimes had to listen while sitting outside. The southern states of the USA were split by racism at this time. Whites were often banned from African-American areas. But Elvis was not put off and watched how the ministers and choirs would use their bodies to keep time with the beat and emphasize the underlying message of the words.

In 1941 the USA entered the **Second World War**. The need for aircraft, tanks, guns and other weapons to be used in the war meant more and better paid jobs, even in small towns like East Tupelo. Vernon had a steady job for the first time in his life. He used the money to buy a second-hand Plymouth car and

Segregation

Throughout most of the first half of this century the southern states of the USA (and some northern states) practised segregation of the races. African-Americans and whites not only went to different churches, they sat in different parts of buses, sat on different park benches and even used different drinking fountains. African-Americans were refused entry to many restaurants and theatres.

a radio, on which Elvis got to hear **country music**, swing and other new styles, in particular the rhythm and blues performed by African-American musicians. With the extra income, Gladys had $10 to spend on Elvis's eleventh birthday present. She bought a guitar and persuaded Elvis's Uncle Luther to give the boy lessons.

To Memphis

In September 1948 Vernon was arrested for selling illegal whisky. The local magistrate ordered him to leave Mississippi and never return. Elvis later recalled: 'We left Tupelo overnight.

Elvis aged about eight, with his father, Vernon Presley, and mother, Gladys. Dad packed all our belongings in boxes and put them on the top and in the trunk of our Plymouth. Then we headed for Memphis.' Memphis, Tennessee, was a large industrial city of 300,000 people. At first the country boy Elvis found the city intimidating and daunting.

FIRST SONGS

A teenage Elvis in fancy dress. During his teen years, Elvis loved dressing in unusual clothes.

In Memphis, Vernon got a job in a factory while Gladys worked as a waitress. Together they earned just $35 a week and could only afford to rent a one-room apartment. In 1949 Elvis went to the L C Humes High School, which gave a solid education to poor children so that they could get good honest jobs.

One girl at L C Humes recalled Elvis: 'He was a very shy person, but he did carry this guitar with him.' Elvis played the guitar in breaks and between lessons to entertain his friends, one of whom was Red West, a tough member of the school football team, who shared Elvis's liking for modern music. Elvis liked to visit Beale Street, in Memphis, where he could listen to African-American musicians who influenced his own style of music so much.

A NEW LOOK

In the autumn of 1950 Elvis got a part-time job, earning $12.60 for working 25 hours a week selling tickets and popcorn and showing people to their seats at the Loew's

State **Theater**. Most of the money went to help pay the family's bills, but Elvis kept some to spend on outrageous clothes. Pink shirts and black trousers were a favourite outfit and Elvis also grew his hair long, slicked back with hair oil. This glamorous new look did Elvis no good at school, where he was picked on by other boys. One day three of them cornered Elvis and threatened to cut his hair short, but Red West turned up and frightened the boys off.

Elvis with his parents in 1954. Elvis was just beginning to enjoy success at this time.

In December 1952 Elvis was talked into taking part in the school show by the history teacher Miss Scrivener. Elvis walked on with his old guitar in his hand. 'Then it happened,' said Red West, 'Elvis put one foot up on a chair to act as a prop, and he started to plunk away. When he finished, the kids went crazy. Elvis seemed to be amazed that for the first time in his life someone other than his family really liked him. As shy as he was, he had a definite magic on stage.'

'Elvis stood out like a camel in the Arctic.'
Fellow High School pupil

Elvis the truck driver

When Elvis left school in June 1953 his family was still short of money, so he took a job as a poorly paid truck driver for the Crown Electric Company. At the time he told a friend: 'I don't need that much money, just enough for me and Mama to get by.'

The birthday present

In August 1953, Elvis decided to cut a cheap record of himself singing a song as a birthday present for his mother. He walked into the Sun Studios of the Memphis Recording Service where he could record his voice for just $4. The studio assistant, Marion Keisker, thought Elvis had real singing talent, so she made a tape of part of the recording.

Sun Studios was run by Sam Phillips, who ran a small **record label** that sold songs by local bands to the southern market. On 26 June 1954 Phillips suddenly needed a singer at short notice. He had

Elvis's style

'I sing all kinds. I don't sound like nobody', Elvis said in reply to Marion Keisker when she asked what style of music he sang. She was setting levels in the recording studio and needed to know if he would be crooning (soft) or playing loud. He misunderstood and thought she meant music style, hence the reply.

The Sun Studios in Memphis, Tennessee, where Elvis cut his first disc and where he signed his first recording deal. Marion Keisker call Presley and ask him to come in for a trial recording. 'I ran all the way', Elvis remembered. 'I was there by the time they hung up the phone.' Phillips later said, 'Man, this was just Elvis on a guitar, and he could wail the heck out of a guitar. I heard him and that was it.' Phillips got in touch with professional musicians he thought would work well with Elvis.

Sun Records

○ Sun Records had recorded well-known African-American blues musicians before, but southern whites never bought

○ such records. Phillips always hoped one day to find a white singer who sounded like a African-American singer to help

○ this vibrant music get across to a white audience.

Sun Records

At the urging of Sam Phillips, Elvis Presley teamed up with country guitarist Scotty Moore and bass player Bill Black to form the Hillbilly Cats. On 6 July 1954 the trio went to Sun Studios to record a few tracks. The first two songs were not up to much, but then Elvis began thumping out 'That's All Right, Mama'. Phillips was startled and ran through to the studio. 'What the devil are you boys doing?', he demanded. 'Don't know,' replied Elvis. 'Well find out real quick', shouted Phillips, 'and let's put it on tape.'

A recording session at Sun Studios with, from left to right, Elvis Presley, Bill Black, Scotty Moore and Sam Phillips.

The song was recorded for release as a single and was in the shops just twelve days later. Phillips took it to WHBQ, a Memphis radio station that had a rhythm and blues show called *Red Hot and Blue*. The DJ, Dewey Phillips, agreed to play the disc. One schoolmate of Elvis recalled the evening clearly: 'My mom was all excited and called out to me to come in and listen to the radio as a boy from my school was singing. I knew it had to be Elvis. He was the only one whose singing was worth a damn.' 'That's All Right, Mama' reached number three in the Memphis Country charts in July 1954.

THE NEW STAR

As the record played, Dewey Phillips got so many calls from the public that he wanted to have Elvis in the studio. He called Sun Studios and Sam Phillips raced round to Elvis's home, only to find the new star had gone out to the movies. When Elvis eventually got to the studio he chatted nervously to the DJ, only to discover afterwards that he had been live on air. He almost fainted.

Elvis signed a recording contract with Sun Records, while Scotty Moore took charge of the live performances. Elvis wore an outrageous pink and white cowboy outfit and, because he and Moore were from Memphis, they tended to be billed as a **country music** act. But their thumping music and Elvis's gyrating dancing was unlike any other country music act, and it sent the young people in the audience wild. Elvis had managed to combine the feel and sounds of African-American music with the tunes and lyrics of white music. Because he was white himself he was more acceptable to the music industry than many talented African-Americans.

A second opinion

In September 1954, Moore booked Elvis into Nashville's Grand Ole Opry, the biggest venue in Tennessee, for their first live radio broadcast. Unfortunately the audience was older than those who appreciated Elvis, and the new band went down badly. Jim Denny, the Opry's manager, told Elvis, 'Listen boy, you should quit singing and go back to driving a truck.'

Elvis decided he would give up music after playing one more booking, a radio show called the *Louisiana Hayride*. But the younger *Hayride* audience reacted enthusiastically to Elvis and the band was offered a regular contract at $42 a time. Next day, Elvis handed in his notice at his job. Soon the band was playing almost every night at county fairs, bars and clubs.

During this time Elvis built up a massive fan base in the southern states. The appeal of the young singer

Elvis the Pelvis

During his early appearances on stage, Elvis swung his hips in time to the music in a fashion no other singer had ever used. In anatomy, the pelvis is part of the hip, so newspapers started calling him 'Elvis the Pelvis'. At first, Elvis himself did not realize that it was partly his dance style that made him so popular. Talking about one appearance he said: 'My manager told me that the audience was hollering because I was wiggling. And so I went out for an encore, and I wiggled a little more. And the more I did the wilder they went.'

was partly his good looks and flashy clothes, but the main attractions were the great music and the extraordinary dance style which earned him the nickname 'Elvis the Pelvis'.

Elvis also had a new type of fan. Previously, young people had left school aged twelve or fourteen to get a job and only the wealthy went on to college, but in the 1950s more young people stayed on at school and took only part-time jobs. They had spending money, but none of the responsibilities of adults. They were called 'teenagers'.

'You know if that young man keeps going like that he's going to make it real big one of these days.'
Singer Slim Whitman, 1954

THE COLONEL

In May 1955, Elvis and the band joined the Hank Snow **Jamboree** tour. The tour brought Elvis to a new audience and demand for his next single, 'Mystery Train', boomed. The tour was also critical in another way. Working for the Jamboree was **publicist** and manager **Colonel** Tom Parker. He spotted Elvis as a major talent and decided to take the boy on. The partnership was to last until Elvis's death.

COLONEL PARKER

orn Andreas Cornelius van Kuijk in the
Netherlands, **Colonel** Tom Parker moved to
the USA as a young man and
spent some time in the army
before joining a travelling carnival.
He changed his name to something
easier to pronounce and became a
full-time publicist and **promoter**.
After meeting Elvis Presley during
the 1955 **Jamboree** tour, Parker
offered to handle all the business
and promotional side of Elvis's
career for 25 per cent of everything Elvis made.
Parker told Elvis, 'You stay young and sexy and I'll
make us both rich as **rajahs**.'

Elvis and his
manager, Colonel
Tom Parker. Elvis
signed his
contract with
Parker in August
1955.

The Colonel put together a record deal that would
make Elvis rich and famous. Ignoring offers from
market leaders Columbia-CBS and Atlantic, he went
for RCA. The company already put out
records by Hank Snow and Eddie
Arnold, also managed by the Colonel,
and he trusted them. The deal was
finalized on 20 November 1955. RCA
paid $40,000. Elvis took his money and
rushed out to buy his mother a flashy
pink **Cadillac** limousine.

'When I met him, he
had a million dollars
worth of talent.
Now he's got a
million dollars.'
Colonel Tom Parker

A FAST BUCK

Throughout the partnership, Elvis and Parker achieved staggering success, but were often criticized by music businessmen for being more interested in money than artistic merit. Often Parker insisted that songwriters gave Elvis a cut of their **royalties** before he would sing their songs, or he forced Elvis to perform on stage when he was far from well. In truth, neither Parker nor Elvis really believed the fame and fortune would last very long. By the time they realized Elvis was an established star, they had become so accustomed to making money fast that they could not break the habit.

'He can't last. I tell you flat. He can't last.'
Jackie Gleason, TV producer, 1956

The first recording session at RCA produced one of his greatest hits: 'Heartbreak Hotel'. The track blended the raw energy Elvis used on the road with the skill and smoothness of the professional RCA musicians and sound engineers. The single was released on 27 January 1956. By the end of March it was number one on the **Billboard** Popular Music Chart and the **Country Music** Chart and number five on the Rhythm and Blues Chart. This marked Elvis as a performer to watch.

NATIONAL TELEVISION

Meanwhile, Parker had booked Presley and the band to appear on television's nationally broadcast *Stage Show,* hosted by Tommy and Jimmy Dorsey, for a fee of $1250. Elvis wore black trousers and shirt with a white tie, specially designed to look good on black and white television. The audience was packed with teenagers and when Elvis sang, they went wild, guaranteeing Elvis an instant return booking.

Next, Parker persuaded television's *Milton Berle Show* to part with $10,000 for a two-show deal. Elvis performed the gyrating dances which were so popular on stage, but they did not go down well with a middle-aged television audience. Over 700,000 letters of complaint flooded in to Milton Berle.

Elvis and his band on stage practising for *The Ed Sullivan Show,* which was to take his musical style to a national audience.

On 9 September 1956 Elvis appeared on *The Ed Sullivan Show.* This time **Colonel** Parker negotiated a fee of $50,000 and the show broke all records for **ratings**. Fifty-four million people, some 82 per cent of all television-watching Americans, tuned in to see Elvis rock through 'Don't Be Cruel', 'Hound Dog' and 'Love Me Tender'. A second appearance came on 28 October, but the third show on 6 January 1957 caused controversy.

Sullivan had also received many complaint letters about Elvis's act and his dancing, so he decided Elvis could only be shown from the waist up. This was designed to mask Presley's gyrations and stop complaints, but Elvis refused to change an act so popular with live audiences just for the television cameras. He danced with renewed energy, while the studio audience screamed and cheered louder than ever. Then Elvis decided to use his arms to make up for the fact his legs could not be seen. The performance was electrifying and seemed guaranteed to lead to new heights of controversy.

'SAFE' AGAIN

However, Ed Sullivan had taken to Elvis during rehearsals. He put his own reputation at risk by saying on screen, 'I wanted to say to Elvis Presley and the country that this is a real decent fine boy, and we've never had a pleasanter experience on our show with a big name than we've had with him. You're thoroughly all right.' Elvis was thrilled as he had never wanted or deserved a bad reputation. Colonel Parker was thrilled as well. His star act was 'safe' again and could be booked into more profitable shows.

To Hollywood

A poster for the first Elvis movie, *Love Me Tender*. Originally conceived as a dramatic western, the movie was hurriedly rewritten as a musical when Elvis was cast.

In the spring of 1956 the **movie producer** Hal Wallis, of Paramount Pictures, saw Elvis perform on *Stage Show*. Won over by the show, Wallis rang **Colonel** Parker and arranged for Elvis to fly to Hollywood for a screen test. Elvis delivered a few lines of dramatic script. Wallis must have been impressed as Paramount Pictures immediately offered Elvis a three-movie deal worth $450,000.

However, his first movie was actually for 20th Century Fox, who 'borrowed' Elvis from Paramount. The movie, a dramatic western starring established Hollywood favourites Richard Egan and Debra Paget, was at first called *The Reno Brothers*, but was renamed *Love Me Tender* after the song Elvis sang in the movie. Unlike some temperamental stars, Elvis was always on time and knew his lines.

When the movie opened in New York on 15 November 1956 a vast crowd of teenagers turned out. Police had to block the road and clear a path for the celebrities and press photographers. In less than a week the film turned a profit – nobody in Hollywood could remember a movie having such box-office success before. Paramount immediately recognized a money-spinner and put Elvis into the starring role of *Loving You*, in which he played a character similar to his own, a poor boy who makes a fortune as a singer. He sang eight songs in this movie one of which, 'Teddy Bear', was released as a single and hit number one.

GRACELAND

In February 1957, Elvis had a bad scare. He was getting out of his car at home when a group of teenage fans leapt at him and tore his clothes off for souvenirs. Vernon Presley dashed out and pulled Elvis clear. The Presleys decided they had to move to a house with a wall around the grounds. The money from the movie contracts gave them the cash to buy a large mansion in Memphis named Graceland, set in a 6-hectare garden. They totally redecorated the house, equipping it with powerful air conditioning and a racquet ball court. The main entrance was torn down and replaced with the famous Music Gate – iron gates featuring musical notes and a guitar-playing Elvis. Worried that fans who pushed against the gates might be hurt, Elvis insisted that there should be no sharp edges on the metalwork.

Meanwhile, Elvis called on Red West to act as a bodyguard. Soon Marty Lacker had joined Elvis to make sure transport was always laid on and that Elvis arrived on time. Sonny West, Red's brother, and Lamar Fike were hired to help out with security and bag-carrying. Together these four old school friends formed a vital support group for Elvis and were soon known as the 'Memphis Mafia'.

THE GOLDEN BOY

Elvis's next movie was *Jailhouse Rock*. He received 50 per cent of studio profits as well as his fee of $250,000. Elvis was allowed to arrange the songs and dance routines himself, and he took full advantage of the opportunity. The most spectacular sequence in the movie is the dance routine to the title song: the stark black and white images of jail bars and a line of convict dancers is one of the most enduring images of 1950s' rock music. But the added responsibility had its drawbacks. Elvis had to show

Suit of gold

One of Presley's most famous 1950s outfits was a dinner suit made of gold lamé material. But he did not like it very much and often wore only the jacket. Eventually, **Colonel** Parker borrowed it and wore it more often than Elvis himself.

up for work at 7.30am and rarely left the set before 6pm. By the end of shooting, the star was exhausted.

Meanwhile, the venues Elvis played for his live shows grew bigger and more profitable as the months passed. In the recording studio he went back to his musical roots with a number of gospel songs, followed by 'The Elvis Christmas Album', a collection of numbers that ranged from **rock and roll** to seasonal children's songs and hymns.

A dramatic still from the movie Jailhouse Rock, *which was shot in 1957 and featured Elvis singing no fewer than thirteen songs.*

His next movie revealed Elvis's talent as an actor. In *King Creole* he plays a sombre, violent character who works in the seedy nightclubs of New Orleans. Elvis acted well and the film received good **reviews**, mostly due to the director Michael Curtiz and **Oscar** nominee co-stars Walter Matthau and Carolyn Jones.

GI BLUE

When Elvis was at the height of his fame, fate dealt him a blow. The 23-year-old Elvis was called up before the next **draft** board to serve in the military. **Colonel** Parker worked out a deal with the army under which Elvis was allowed a 60-day delay to finish his movie and recording work before showing up for induction into the army on 24 March 1958.

THE MILITARY AND THE MEDIA

Most people expected Elvis to try to avoid the draft or to go for a soft option playing music for the troops, but, determined not to demand or take special privileges, Elvis refused. He was given the **dog tag** number 53310761 before being sent off for six months' basic training at Fort Hood, in Texas. The media were allowed to film Elvis's first day in minute detail. The cutting of his famous long hair to the regulation **crew cut** was a press sensation. When it became obvious that Elvis had behaved like a patriotic boy, putting his career on hold to serve his country, many of his critics were won over. Elvis lost his bad boy image.

The draft
In 1950s' America, and in many other countries, too, young men could be 'drafted' or 'called up' for compulsory military service. Draftees could put off being drafted by going to college. If they were married with children, they could avoid the draft altogether.

'It's tough living up to an image.'
Elvis Presley

Colonel Parker did not want Elvis to emerge from the army two years later to find his career was over, so he persuaded Elvis to spend his leave recording **rock and roll** tracks. Together with the old Sun Studios songs, Parker had enough music to keep the adoring Elvis fans happy for many months. Only time would tell if they would remain loyal to a star they could no longer see on stage or on screen. Asked if he would continue recording songs during his time in the army, Presley replied, 'I'm in the army. That's my job now.'

GRIEVING

In August 1958 Elvis's mother collapsed and she died a few weeks later. Elvis was devastated and for the rest of his life he found it difficult to talk about her. After twenty days of compassionate leave, Elvis was sent to Germany to join the US troops stationed there. When the troopship docked at Bremerhaven on 1 October 1958 it was met by a large crowd. As soon as Elvis appeared, the crowd surged forward with such force the military police had trouble holding them back.

Elvis in his army uniform. Apart from a few carefully managed photo calls for the press, Elvis stayed out of the limelight during his tour of duty and concentrated on his army role.

'He was an extremely pleasant, sincere young man who took the time and trouble to speak to everyone he met.'
Major Ed Miller, US military base commander

PROMOTION

Elvis was given the task of maintaining, driving and being responsible for a **jeep**. His early love of cars made this as much a hobby as a job. He was frequently sent around Germany driving officers or delivering packages and messages. A surprise inspection of the 4th Armored Division showed that Presley's was one of the few vehicles to achieve top grades for care and maintenance. Elvis became a corporal soon afterwards and later a sergeant.

PRISCILLA BEAULIEU

Elvis found one old friend at his base in Germany: Captain Keisker was the father of Marion Keisker, receptionist at Sun Studios. Keisker introduced Elvis to Captain Joseph Beaulieu, who had a step-daughter named Priscilla. Elvis and Priscilla soon became close, but the girl was only fourteen and Captain Beaulieu laid strict conditions about when and how often the two could meet.

The teenage Priscilla Beaulieu writes a letter to Elvis after his return to the USA. The two dated in Germany for some weeks.

The album cover 'Elvis Is Back!', which refers to him being back from the army, shows the star in a glamorous pose.

Meanwhile, Parker and Elvis began planning moves to relaunch Elvis's career following his **discharge** in March 1960. It was decided to release a movie called *GI Blues* based on Elvis's time in the army. To speed up production, the scenes without Elvis in them were shot before he left the army. Songs for a new album were written and arranged and a recording studio was booked for three weeks after his discharge.

On 1 March, Elvis left Germany and Priscilla came to the airport to wave him goodbye. The newspaper reporters were staggered as it was the first anyone outside the army knew of the romance. Priscilla soon became famous as 'the girl Elvis left behind', but neither she nor Elvis spoke publicly about the romance. After a quick stop-over in Scotland to refuel the aircraft, Elvis flew to the USA for his discharge. The army was happy to go along with the various interviews and press calls arranged by **Colonel** Parker, as they were eager to show that being **drafted** was not the nightmare some young men thought it to be.

'Elvis died when he went into the army.'
    John Lennon, former member of the Beatles

THE FILM YEARS

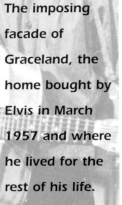

The Graceland to which Elvis returned in 1960 was very largely his creation. The lounge had a graceful charm, with a grand piano and dark blue curtains edged in gold. Carpeted in pure white, the dining room featured a large black marble central panel on which stood the dining table and chairs. The music room, decorated in red, was where Elvis would experiment with tunes, working out the styles and arrangements that suited him and his voice best. In the basement was the famous Jungle Room furnished with Hawaiian footstools and half-moon shaped thrones two metres high covered in

The sumptuously decorated dining room at Graceland which, like all the rooms in the mansion, was personally designed by Elvis.

fur and decorated with wooden carvings of ancient gods. Elvis had the floor and ceiling covered in thick, dark-green carpet, and one entire wall was occupied by a stone sculpture down which water ran and from which plants grew, re-creating a stream tumbling down into a densely forested chasm.

BACK TO WORK

No sooner was Elvis back at Graceland than Parker took him to Nashville to record songs, and at once it was clear to all concerned that Elvis had lost none of his magic, indeed he had grown more dynamic and mature in style. Elvis also flew to Florida to record a television show titled *Welcome Home Elvis*. The **GI** *Blues* movie was released in October and was a hit, which encouraged Paramount to put their next Elvis movie into the cinemas as quickly as possible.

THE WRONG CHOICE

Flaming Star was released in December. There were only two songs and the story dealt with the subject of racial discrimination, with Elvis as a mixed-race Indian living with his white father's family in the old west. This was not the romantic story that Elvis fans wanted to see and, despite the fact that Elvis gave his best movie performance yet, it failed to attract the movie-goers.

FORMULA FOR SUCCESS

Colonel Parker and Elvis duly took note. *Blue Hawaii* saw Elvis sing fourteen songs in a beautiful location, while playing a poor young musician who eventually makes good. The Elvis fans flocked to see

Elvis and his co-stars in a publicity shot for the movie *Blue Hawaii*, released in 1961 and the most successful of all the movies in which Elvis starred.

their hero back on musical form, while the exotic locations and top-rank co-stars guaranteed a good-looking and popular film. It lacked the raw power of *Jailhouse Rock* but was amazingly successful at the box-office. It is, perhaps, the classic Elvis movie and Parker and the Hollywood bosses decided to follow the same formula in future – Elvis would be paid $1 million per movie, plus a share of the profits.

Elvis had dated several girls since returning from Germany, but none had lasted long. At Christmas 1960 he invited Priscilla to visit. Captain Beaulieu had read newspaper reports about Elvis's relationships as much as anyone else, and consented to this and later visits only after Elvis agreed to a **chaperone**. In May 1962 Priscilla turned eighteen, and her step-father relented, allowing Priscilla to come and live at Graceland while she finished her schooling.

In 1966 Elvis recorded the album 'How Great Thou Art', which won him his first **Grammy** award. But most of his efforts went into the movies, sometimes completing three a year. However, big changes were taking place in the pop world. The Beatles, Rolling Stones and other groups were experimenting with new forms of music. Elvis, who still put out music of the 1950s, was left behind. Recognizing the real danger that he could fade away as a star, Elvis decided on a new direction to his career.

THE COMEBACK

The decision by Elvis to relaunch his career may have had much to do with his personal life. In May 1967 he married Priscilla in a private ceremony at the Aladdin Hotel in Las Vegas. Elvis was dressed in a dark brocade **tuxedo** and sported a white carnation. Priscilla had her hair in a fashionable bouffant style, and dyed black to match Elvis, while her dress was a loose gown with beaded lace over the arms and shoulders. It was a surprisingly modest event with only a handful of family guests. There was, however, a showy six-tiered cake festooned with red roses and sugar hearts for the press call.

The extravagant cake baked for the wedding of Elvis and Priscilla, which took place in Las Vegas on 1 May 1967.

NEW BEGINNINGS

Priscilla gave birth to their daughter, Lisa Marie, in Memphis the following February. Elvis proved to be a devoted father, making time in his busy schedule

for their new child, and his increased happiness and enthusiasm for life spurred him on to look for new projects.

He had gone to the RCA Studios in Nashville for a major recording session the previous September – simply trying out ideas and arrangements rather than recording for either a film or an album. Having not performed live for years, he was understandably nervous about going on stage again. In the end Elvis decided on a recorded television show with a live audience, scheduled for Christmas 1968 on NBC. The format would allow any mistakes to be edited out before the show was transmitted.

Elvis and Priscilla with their daughter at the photo shoot on 5 February 1968 when the press and public got their first view of the newborn baby.

'As the years went by I missed audience contact', Elvis said. 'I was really getting bugged. I couldn't do what I could do, y'know. They (film directors) would say "action" and I would go "uh-uh".'

THE '68 SPECIAL

The show's producer, Steve Binder, saw it as a way to relaunch the energy and power of Elvis's 1950s stage shows. The idea was that several big-set numbers would begin and end the show, with a centre slot when Elvis and his band would appear on a small stage surrounded by a live audience. **Colonel** Parker thought it too risky and wanted Elvis simply to sing a few songs and a Christmas hymn or two. Elvis backed Binder.

But the centre slot, with a live audience, had Elvis deeply worried. Trying out some of his stage movements, he found himself extremely out of breath, so he began a strict diet and exercise routine to get fit. But without a live audience it was difficult to know how successful the act would be. Elvis was visibly shaking when he finally strode out on to the stage, but the show turned out to be a triumph with Elvis on top form. Scotty Moore, not having performed with Elvis for some time, was most impressed. 'In the '68 Special he was just as much like he was in the first years, '54 or '55, as you could ask him to be,' Moore said later.

'He gave everything that he had – more than anyone knew he had.'
Critic Greil Marcus, on the 1968 TV show

After weeks of editing, cutting and re-recording of some songs, the finished Special was ready for broadcast on 3 December 1968. It was the session

Elvis on stage in his black leather jump suit for the central section of his 1968 Television Special. Many critics thought it was the best part of the show.

with a live audience that relaunched Elvis's career. Dressed in an all-black leather jump suit, at first Elvis gyrated around alone to re-create his 1950s dance style. Then the band came on stage and sat on stools with him. Elvis chatted to the audience, bringing them in on the act. They loved it, and the fans at home were thrilled to see a new, more dynamic Elvis.

His confidence boosted, a marathon recording session followed and Elvis became a popular major rock star again. But Elvis now wanted one more go at being an actor, and he chose to star in a western, *Charro*. There was no music in the movie and Elvis further surprised his fans by growing a beard for the part. *Charro* did not do well and Elvis gave up any idea of being a serious actor after that.

THE VEGAS YEARS

Having had great success on television and with records, Elvis wanted to go back to where he started – touring with a live show. **Colonel** Parker decided that, in order to cope with the huge number of fans, Elvis should only play venues large enough to hold thousands of people. He was looking for somewhere suitable when the International Hotel in Las Vegas offered Elvis a massive $1 million for a four-week appearance.

SHOWTIME

In July 1969 Elvis flew to Las Vegas to start rehearsals with the band with which he would appear. On 31 July he went back on stage. The act

As the years passed, Elvis took to wearing impressive white suits with turned-up collars and flared trousers. They became a trademark that has been copied by many imitators since.

opened with a dark stage, suddenly illuminated by a single spotlight into which stepped Elvis just as the band burst into life. Elvis was dressed in an entirely new style. No longer wearing casual clothes, he wore a jet black suit with flared sleeves and high collar, an outfit that gradually developed over the coming months into the glittering jumpsuits which became an Elvis hallmark. He also began to practise some moves that became typical in later shows: he would kneel down at the front of the stage to talk to or touch the first few rows of fans, and towards

the end of the act would ask for a
handkerchief, use it to wipe his face,
and hand it back.

The shows were booked solid and the
hotel asked Elvis to stay for a further
two weeks, then return again the
following year. When he returned for
60 days in 1970 the number of tourists visiting Las
Vegas rocketed – the city council estimated that
profits from gambling, drinks and food rose by 10
per cent when Elvis was in town.

ON THE ROAD

Leaving Las Vegas, Elvis started a gruelling tour of
American cities, beginning with the Houston
Astrodome in Texas where the enormous profit
finally convinced Parker that Elvis could make as
much money touring as in the movies. He extended
the tour and persuaded Elvis to spend nearly all his
time on the road. Over the next seven years, Elvis
was to visit 125 cities and play over a thousand
concerts, an average of three per week, every one
of them sold out.

SUCCESS WORLDWIDE

Although Elvis had decided not to make any more
musical movies, he could not ignore the film
business entirely. In December 1970 he starred in

Elvis – That's the Way It Is. Unlike his earlier films, this was a documentary about Elvis on tour. It was a huge success with those who could not get to see him live, especially abroad.

And the hit records continued to pour out, but the greatest achievement of Elvis's comeback happened in 1973 when *Elvis: Aloha from Hawaii*, a televised concert held to raise funds for cancer research, was broadcast from the Hawaiian islands. Audiences in Japan, South Korea, Australia, New Zealand, Vietnam, Thailand and the Philippines were able to see the show live, while time differences meant that those in Europe had to wait until the following day.

THE END

Elvis, Priscilla and Lisa in one of the last photos taken of them as a family. Despite the divorce, Elvis remained devoted to his daughter.

Even though Elvis was enjoying massive success in the early 1970s, his personal life was in trouble. The constant touring insisted upon by **Colonel** Parker was a strain and Elvis did not see Priscilla as often as he would have liked. In October 1973, after six years of marriage, they were divorced. Lisa Marie was only five then, but her parents remained friends, and Priscilla became a frequent visitor to Graceland or to wherever Elvis happened to be on tour.

In 1976, RCA pressured Elvis into recording some entirely new songs. The concerts remained sell-outs, but were largely made up of old favourites and did not help sell records. Trying to avoid the task, Elvis came up with excuse after excuse, only agreeing after RCA said he could record the songs in a mobile studio at Graceland. The session produced a group of songs that varied from outstanding to mediocre, but the album sold well.

Health problems

Unknown to his fans, Elvis was becoming seriously ill. Early in 1974 Elvis failed to appear on a television gospel show due to 'ill health'. On several occasions he slipped into the Baptist Hospital in Memphis to be treated for exhaustion, eye strain or **pneumonia**. But the most worrying health problems were to do with his diet. From childhood, Elvis had been devoted to southern country cooking, such as grits, corn pone, fried corn and okra and biscuits, as well as deep-fried sandwiches – designed for hard-working farmers, not singers who spent days sitting around. Elvis would pile on weight to reach 102 kg (16 stone), then go on a crash diet before going on stage.

Matters were made worse by his increasing reliance on drugs. Although the drugs were legal, Elvis took them in reckless quantities. He took sleeping pills and stimulants to cope with the stress on the road, then appetite suppressants to help his crash diets and laxatives to cope with the sudden return to binge eating after a stage tour. The drugs were originally prescribed by Elvis's own doctor, who had been treating him since 1966. At first, he encouraged Elvis to exercise regularly and curb his craving for fat-laden dishes. But in the early 1970s the doctor gave up the struggle and he, and various other doctors, began signing prescriptions for quantities of drugs that were later thought dangerously unwise.

FINAL MONTHS

By the summer of 1976 Elvis was visibly ill, although the cause was not public knowledge. One critic wrote: 'Elvis strode on stage puffy faced and dressed in a gaudy costume with a six-inch belt, he posed for thousands of instamatic flashcubes during a quick run through of "CC Rider". He still has a remarkably strong, deeply resonant voice that, unfortunately, he displayed only rarely. He spent most of his time tossing scarves like Mardi Gras favours to the audience, shaking hands, receiving flowers and presents and kissing the women persistent enough to break through the throng to the stage and pull themselves up close enough to the King that he didn't have to lean over too far.'

In March 1977 Elvis was forced to cut short a tour and was rushed to hospital. He was able to resume the tour the following month, but he was by then clearly very ill. On the night of 15 August 1977, Elvis could not sleep. He sat down at his piano to play some old favourites. Sometime after dawn he stopped playing and picked up a religious book. A few hours later he was found slumped on the bathroom floor. He was rushed to the Baptist Hospital but to no avail.

'I wouldn't have cared if they had to wheel him out in a wheelbarrow – it was still Elvis.'
Scott Rohde (fan talking about a late 1976 concert)

Elvis on the stage in a dramatic suit first seen in 1975. By this date his health was suffering and he sometimes appeared puffy and out of breath on stage.

At 3.30pm he was pronounced dead. The immediate cause of death was heart failure, but exactly what underlying causes led up to the failure were not stated on the death certificate and have been the subject of debate ever since.

THE LEGEND LIVES ON

Crowds line the streets to watch the funeral cortege of Elvis Presley as it winds through the streets of Memphis on 18 August 1977.

The news that Elvis was dead spread quickly. By 6.30pm a crowd of over 20,000 people had gathered outside Graceland. They stood silently in shocked surprise. A reporter recalled the moment the news arrived: 'I was visiting the *Chicago Sun-Times* … when a guy ran by yelling, "Elvis is dead!" Seconds later a voice boomed across the newsroom, "Stop the presses". It was a moment I'd only seen in the movies. To this day, I still get chills when I think of that editor ordering the *Sun-Times*'s presses to stop.'

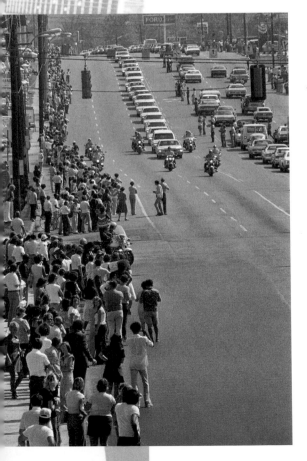

A PRESIDENT PAYS TRIBUTE

The funeral was held two days later at Forest Hills Cemetery, Memphis, where Gladys Presley was buried. Over 200,000 people turned up to line the route. US President Jimmy Carter paid an official tribute when he said, 'Elvis Presley's death deprives our country of a part of itself. He was a symbol to the people of the world of the vitality, rebelliousness and good humour of this country.'

Elvis was dead, but his adoring fans would not let the legend of the King of **Rock and Roll** die with him. So many people visited the grave that the bodies of both Elvis and his mother had to be transferred to a private plot in the grounds of Graceland. Across the world fans set up **posthumous** fan clubs and began creating their own memorials to the King.

The private burial plot at Graceland.

REMEMBERING ELVIS

Elvis left most of his possessions and the rights to his work to his daughter, Lisa Marie, with Priscilla as trustee until Lisa Marie reached 25 years of age. Priscilla Presley decided to devote her life to safeguarding the memory of Elvis and ensuring that her daughter had a secure inheritance. She declared, 'I don't want Lisa, when she's 25, to say "Where's my Dad's stuff?" '

Priscilla created Elvis Presley Enterprises and invested the $500,000 cash left by Elvis in opening Graceland to the public. The house and grounds were restored to how they had been when Elvis was at the peak of his career. In his will, Elvis also declared that any members of his family who wanted to live at Graceland could do so, and some still do.

Today, Graceland is the second most visited property open to the public in the USA, with over 600,000 visitors a year. Only the President's White House is more popular. On show are the original 1955 pink **Cadillac** that Elvis bought his mother with his first big payment, together with the Cadillac with the customized gold-plated dashboard that Elvis drove the day before he died.

THE LEGEND

Even in the new millennium the Elvis legend lives on. When Elvis died there were 38 Elvis impersonators who earned money singing his songs at private parties or appearing at charity events. Today there are an estimated 11,000. Paramount has released many of its more popular Elvis musicals on home video and thousands have been sold. Even the toy manufacturers have got in on the act,

Elvis Presley impersonators take part in an Elvis Contest in Bangkok.

with Barbie being produced with a special Elvis doll. The records continue to sell in vast numbers, with more than one billion having been sold worldwide. The exact figure is impossible to calculate as some countries have not kept detailed figures, but even so Elvis is the top-selling artist of all time: while Elvis has over 100 platinum or gold discs, the second most popular act, the Beatles, has just 45.

More startling than the continuing success of Elvis records and memorabilia is the persistent legend that Elvis did not die. It was thought that maybe Elvis had retreated from the pressures of worldwide stardom to retire to a quiet hideaway somewhere.

One early witness reported, 'I saw Elvis in at the local diner down here in Overbrook. He was drinking a diet coke and eating some fried chicken. When he left he thanked the cook for a mighty good meal and said he sure was thankful. He paid with a hundred dollar bill and told her to keep the change. He then got in a 1953 Chevy Bel-Air custom turquoise and white auto. It had tinted windows and he said to the driver "Let's go, Bubba", and he was gone.' Similar sightings have been reported more recently in Dublin, Ireland, and elsewhere, and will, no doubt, continue to be posted on the Internet as long as the Elvis legend lives on.

THE CHANGING VIEW OF ELVIS

John Lennon said, 'Before Elvis there was nothing.' Elvis said about himself that he was lucky to come into the music industry at the right time, when there was no trend. Both points of view underestimate the phenomenon of Elvis's music. By not being afraid to sound and move like a African-American singer when he sang white tunes and lyrics, he produced a new and unique style that influenced musicians worldwide – Lennon also said: 'If there hadn't been an Elvis, there wouldn't have been the Beatles.'

Many influential people in the United States disliked Elvis early on in his career. Ed Sullivan had said: 'I won't touch Elvis with a long stick' not long before booking him for three shows. Frank Sinatra, a star of a previous generation, said his music was deplorable, others called it 'vulgar' and 'talentless'. The religious leader Billy Graham said that Elvis was not the sort of boy he would like his children to see. After military service, however, and the repackaging of Elvis as the clean-cut all-American boy,

'Elvis Presley is a weapon of the American psychological war aimed at infecting a part of the population with a new outlook of inhumanity.'
Youth World, East German Communist newspaper

Elvis Presley performs with Frank Sinatra in 1960.

he was praised by Sinatra, who sang along with Elvis when he appeared (in evening dress) on the *Frank Sinatra Show*. Gone was the rebel with the long hair and outrageous clothes, and gone too was the Elvis who 'was so different in everything he did'.

With the '68 Special, critics saw a real possibility of the old Elvis returning – 'finding his way back home', as one critic put it – but the concert schedule that followed wrecked his marriage and eventually his health. If Elvis had been a stronger person perhaps he could have handled his fame better, but his childhood poverty probably made it hard for him to quit making money. No doubt Elvis relied on the adoration of his audience as much as he relied on the reckless quantities of drugs he took to get himself through the day.

His death was an international tragedy, but Elvis the rock legend lives on, his position unchallenged. In the words of Bruce Springsteen, 'There have been several contenders, but only one King.'

FILMS AND RECORDS

FILMS

1956	*Love Me Tender* (20th Century Fox)
1957	*Loving You* (Paramount)
	Jailhouse Rock (Metro-Goldwyn-Mayer)
1958	*King Creole* (Paramount)
1960	*GI Blues* (Paramount)
	Flaming Star (Paramount)
1961	*Wild in the Country* (Paramount)
	Blue Hawaii (Paramount)
1962	*Follow That Dream* (Paramount)
	Kid Galahad (Paramount)
	Girls! Girls! Girls! (Paramount)
1963	*Fun in Acapulco* (Paramount)
	It Happened at the World's Fair (Metro-Goldwyn-Mayer)
1964	*Kissin' Cousins* (Paramount)
	Viva Las Vegas (Paramount)
	Roustabout (Paramount)
1965	*Girl Happy* (Paramount)
	Tickle Me (Paramount)
	Harum Scarum (Paramount)
1966	*Paradise, Hawaiian Style* (Paramount)
	Spinout (Metro-Goldwyn-Mayer)
	Frankie and Johnny (United Artists)
1967	*Double Trouble* (Metro-Goldwyn-Mayer)
	Clambake (United Artists)
	Easy Come, Easy Go (Paramount)
1968	*Stay Away Joe* (Metro-Goldwyn-Mayer)
	Speedway (Metro-Goldwyn-Mayer)
	Live a Little, Love a Little (Metro-Goldwyn-Mayer)
1969	*Charro* (National General Pictures)
	The Trouble with Girls (Metro-Goldwyn-Mayer)
	Change of Habit (Metro-Goldwyn-Mayer)
1970	*Elvis – That's the Way It Is* (Metro-Goldwyn-Mayer)
1972	*Elvis on Tour* (Metro-Goldwyn-Mayer)

SINGLES – MILLION-COPY SELLERS

All RCA Recordings

1956
'Heartbreak Hotel'
'I Was the One'
'I Want You, I Need You, I Love You'
'Hound Dog'
'Don't Be Cruel'
'Blue Suede Shoes'
'Love Me Tender'
'Any Way You Want Me'

1957
'All Shook Up'
'That's When Your Heartbreak Begins'
'Teddy Bear'
'Loving You'
'Jailhouse Rock'
'Treat Me Nice'

1958
'Don't'
'I Beg of You'
'One Night'
'Wear My Ring Around Your Neck'
'Hard Headed Woman'
'I Got Stung'

1959
'A Fool Such as I'
'A Big Hunk o' Love'

1960
'Stuck on You'
'It's Now or Never'
'A Mess of Blues'
'Are You Lonesome Tonight?'
'I Gotta Know'

1961
'Surrender'
'I Feel So Bad'

'Little Sister'
'Can't Help Falling in Love'
'Rock-a-Hula Baby'

1962
'She's Not You'
'Return to Sender'
'Where Do You Come From?'

1963
'One Broken Heart for Sale'
'Devil in Disguise'
'Bossa Nova Baby'

1964
'Kissin' Cousins'
'Viva Las Vegas'
'Ain't That Loving You Baby'
'Wooden Heart'

1965
'Crying in the Chapel'
'I'm Yours'

1968
'If I Can Dream'

1969
'In the Ghetto'
'Suspicious Minds'
'Don't Cry Daddy'

1970
'The Wonder of You'

1971
'Kentucky Rain'

1972
'Burning Love'

GLOSSARY

Astrodome a large sports stadium in the city of Houston, Texas

Billboard a magazine which draws up lists of best-selling records in the USA

Cadillac a make of American car famous for luxurious fittings and quality engineering

chaperone someone who accompanies young, unmarried girls on a date

country music a style of music popular in the southeastern states of the USA. It features haunting melodies and sad lyrics about lost love or poverty-stricken rural life.

Colonel a high military rank, but also a title conferred as an honour by some American states. Colonel Tom Parker was an honorary colonel, not a military man.

crew cut a very short hair cut achieved by running electric clippers all over the head

discharge the process of leaving the army, navy or other armed force

dog tag a metal identity tag worn by members of the armed forces

draft two years' military service was compulsory in the US at the time, and all eligible young men were given a number. If your number was chosen, you would be 'drafted'.

GI a soldier in the US Army – short for 'government issue'

gospel a style of Christianity popular among African-American people living in the southern USA, which features powerful preachers and a distinctive style of music

Grammy an award given to singers and songwriters by music industry specialists

Jamboree originally a loud party, but often used to describe a loud stage show

jeep from GP, short for general purpose, a rugged, off-road car used in the US Army

movie producer the person who finds the money and hires the actors, directors and so on for a movie

Oscar an award given to an outstanding actor in a movie

pneumonia a serious disease of the lungs

prescription drugs medicines and drugs that are legal, but are only available if prescribed by a doctor

posthumous after death

promoter a person who starts, finds money for and helps organize something, e.g. a concert or a sports event

publicist a person who organizes publicity, such as adverts, posters and newspaper stories, on behalf of another person

rajah a type of prince in India famous for great wealth and a luxurious lifestyle

ratings an estimate of how many people watch a particular television show. They are important because the amount of money charged for advertisements shown during the programme depends on the size of the ratings.

record label a company which produces music on disc for sale. Record labels often concentrate on producing one type of music, such as classical, country or pop.

review an article in a newspaper or magazine giving an expert opinion of an artistic performance

rock and roll a style of music developed in the 1950s which features drums, guitars and a strong beat

royalties payments made to artists whenever their work is sold or performed

theater usually a cinema where movies are shown, but sometimes a theatre for live shows. (Spelt 'theatre' in the UK.)

tuxedo a formal suit, similar to a dinner suit

Second World War the war fought between 1939 and 1945 with Germany, Japan and their allies on one side and the USA, Britain, Russia and their allies on the other

INDEX